The Gospel of Everyone

The Gospel of Everyone

A poetic retelling of the Gospel of Luke

by Paul Totah

Paul Totah (signature)

Wipf and Stock Publishers

THE GOSPEL OF EVERYONE
A Poetic Retelling of the Gospel of Luke

Resource Publications
An Imprint of Wipf and Stock Publishers
199 W. 8th Ave., Suite 3
Eugene, OR 97401

www.wipfandstock.com

PAPERBACK ISBN: 978-1-5326-1440-8
HARDCOVER ISBN: 978-1-5326-1442-2
EBOOK ISBN: 978-1-5326-1441-5

Manufactured in the U.S.A.   DECEMBER 12, 2016

For Kathryn, my beloved,
& Brian, my friend

Contents

Foreword

In reading Paul Totah's poetic celebrations of characters in the Gospels whom I have known and imagined in much in the same way he has done—following Ignatius of Loyola's special form of imaginative mental prayer, I found myself marveling at Totah's take on each of them, so much like my own in many respects and yet so new and so fresh to me in other ways. I want to say, "I learned so much." But Totah's "teaching" was not like any other. It was the kind of teaching that not only enlightened my mind; it enkindled my heart and triggered in me new flights of imagination. I asked, "Is this how a young John the Baptist could have approached his cousin Jesus?" I'd never asked myself such a question. And now I found myself asking it and answering it with a surprised cry of satisfaction: "Yes, that is the way it had to be." For lovers of Jesus, this is a new kind of treat. Thank you, Paul.

— *Robert Blair Kaiser, author of* Clerical Error *and* Inside the Jesuits: How Pope Fancis is Changing the Church and the World

Paul Totah reads the Gospel of Luke in a poetic version that reveals his own spirituality with very human takes on individual figures and stories. These short poems would be useful for personal meditation, as they draw out our own fears, joys, and longings. Totah puts the well-known gospel into an engaging modern narrative.

— *Eugene Bianchi, Professor of Religion, Emeritus, Emory University*

Preface

This poetic retelling of the Gospel of Luke is not meant to be an account of the historical Christ, one in which I attempt to correct inaccuracies. Nor is it meant to reflect or correct or comment upon Church teaching. I also hope you don't read this looking for answers to questions that have bothered you over the years about your own faith.

These poems are, instead, my attempt to use my human experiences and imagination to touch the humanity of people who lived 2,000 years and 7,000 miles distant from me, whose stories have come to shape my values, my decisions, my work, and my art.

As a student and employee of the Society of Jesus for nearly 40 years, I have taken on the formidable Spiritual Exercises of St. Ignatius of Loyola from time to time, completing the cycle only once, but what a once that was. It taught me to marry my reflection and imagination with meditation and contemplation and to trust in the offsprings of such a union.

These poems are those offsprings. They came from long walks (wanderings) as well as wondering about the backstories of those in the Gospels. Who were these people and how were they drawn to and shaped by Jesus? Reza Aslan's book *Zealot* and my own inconsequential research also colored these poems, but this influence ends in the subtle hues of the coloring.

My hope is that these poems lead you to questions that help you understand more intimately your own loving relationship with yourself, with your neighbor (all of creation included) and with the divinity that links us all. In other words, this is neither history nor dogma — simply my own attempt to live out the great commandment through poetry and to share that journey with you. — *PT*

But there was no information, and so we continued
And arrived at evening, not a moment too soon
Finding the place; it was (you might say) satisfactory.
— T.S. ELIOT, "THE JOURNEY OF THE MAGI"

I. The Beginning

Theophilus

I write this for you
lover of God,
beloved by God,
to tell you the truths,
though I know little first-hand,
and to tell you the truth
that I know by heart.
I have seen only bones
encased in gold
and heard only the echo
of my own voice
praying in darkness and light.
I want to write this story
in the right order, with grace
so that you will know the story
of what you know.
I write this for you, Theophilus.
I write this for myself.

Elizabeth (I)

I thought we were done
with all this nonsense, my womb
as dry as my desire,
not like when we first wed,
you with your thin beard,
I, trying to get used to the scent of a man,
the hunger we had for each other.
I planted a fig tree and grape vines
by the stone wall in front of our house,
just a short walk from Abraham's well,
hoping I could pick fruit with my children
on days when it would be too hot for play.

The fruit never came, only shame and advice
from the crones who told me what to eat,
when to eat, under what moon
to tempt you with perfumes and oils.
I wore my dishonor like a cowl.
It became my home, my purest self,
my shield and my wound:
I could not bear a child.

Years ago, I made peace with this new name:
Barren. I was barren, like a handful of women
who went to the well just for themselves
and their old men whose breasts and buttocks
were as wrinkled and sagging as theirs.

Then you came home, silent as my womb,
but not quiet, gesturing for something with which to write,
weaving a story I could not believe at first,
just as you doubted.
Then I saw your eyes;
I hated the promise you stirred in me.
I did not believe you or anyone could keep it
until you withdrew,

and I knew I was with child.
Still, I endured more stares,
more clucks of tongues,
the well women still disapproving
of someone so old so big with child
out of the swing of time.
Then our boy came wet into the world,
screaming with his small red face
and the midwife questioning
the name I spoke, a name from nowhere,
from an angel, from God himself,
but no one would let me name my son
until my husband wrote:
"His name is John."
Then my husband delivered
his own message, one that had grown nine months in his lungs,
whispering over and over
as he stroked my cheek
and cupped the child's crown:
"Thank you. Thank you. Praise God.
Thank you."

Mary (I)

He came like a flame of grace
shuddering past me
while I picked zucchini in the garden
leaving the fat ones alone
just to see how large they would grow
in the shade of their enormous leaves.
I glanced, then stood, terrified
then not,
barely believing he would speak to me
let alone trusting what he said to be true.
Now, above Ephesus, I wonder why
I wasn't struck dumb like my uncle
when I questioned how this could be:
how a barren woman and a virgin
could awake changed.
At first, I felt the weight of a sycamore
crushing the base of my spine
and then nothing but the breath of a feather,
no weight at all, except the questions
and stares of everyone, the disbelief
of Joseph and, at times, my own doubt
creeping in like the weeds that plagued my garden.
Even now, here among the pines and cold air
of this foreign land, I believe, and don't,
still feel the vanished joy of being a girl
and the peace that followed, a peace that held me
when I clutched his bloody body
at birth and at death.

Elizabeth (II)

This is the story I told my son:
that he leapt in the womb at the first notion
of a cousin to come.
But it was I who leapt.
My heart danced to see you,
another woman bathed in shame,
you for conceiving too soon,
me, for being too late with child.
That's why you stayed until my son was born.
Then you left to prepare for your own time.
I thought this would be easy, raising a son,
something I had seen lesser women do.
But this boy had a thirst for the desert.
He plunged into the hills outside town,
dragging his ancient father at first,
and then going on his own, staying for hours, then days,
making us sick with worry.
He felt more at home with locusts than with boys his age.
On those days, praying for his return,
I recalled what you said to me on that first visit,
and I, too, felt humbled, magnified, blessed, and exalted
for no good reason other than this boy was my son,
my beloved.

Joseph

I noticed the trees on the long march
to Bethlehem as I walked ahead of my wife,
pulling on the donkey's tether.
She carried a child that urged her lungs
closer to her throat with each step the donkey took,
She noticed the children we passed
and wondered how her newborn
would feel to the touch of her hand.
The child would be a boy, she knew,
the way a mother believes and loves
even before seeing.
I saw the stands of pines and thought
what my son might fashion. I wondered if knots
would weaken the grain or form lines
he could learn to read, like his own lineage
leading back to Adam,
a vine of names I had committed to memory.

Later, I felt pained when my own cousins
closed their doors to me and my espoused, still not my wife,
though soon to be the mother of our child.
I would never forget that shame,
nor the certainty when the name
came to me as I held the wailing child
close to my breath and told him: You are Jesus,
son of Joseph of the house of David.
Even beyond death, I will be your father, your abba.
I knelt to kiss Mary's sweating brow;
we two no longer espoused, married now
by blood and child,
by our first journey as family.

The Shepherd

We kept camp in the low hills,
one of us watching for wild dogs, thieves,
and the missing sheep that would lose itself in a ravine.
The rest of us would sleep or gamble,
tell stories about women we never slept with but wished we had,
eat a roasted lamb only when one was too lame or stillborn.
I was sleeping in the tent—
only a blanket thrown over a branch—
when I heard what I cannot describe:
the music of the sky mixed
with shouts of my brothers and son.
The night was lit by some spirit racing and singing,
telling us to wake up, to go to Bethlehem.
Then the heavens were alive,
on fire with a thousand thousand stars,
each dancing in circles, each a candle song
telling us not to fear, to turn our groans
into hosannas, to walk five miles
to a barn to seek a newborn and his parents.
What could we do? I left my own son behind
to watch the flock in case these stars were demons,
and we ran to Bethlehem, to a place we all knew.
The parents were frightened by so many men
crowding their sleep and fatigue with so much noise.
But we had to see, even asked to hold the child,
passing him among us, while we blessed
his scented head with our breath.
We did not run back to the flock, but walked
still seeing the living stars, and then seeing my son
transfixed by the stories he read in the sky,
none of us seeing anything the same any more.

Mary (II)

I never looked forward to going to Jerusalem.
The filth and noise hung in the air
over too many people.
The first two times I passed through its gates brought fear.
The last time, death.
At my son's bris,
I don't know what surprised me more:
Simeon prying my son away,
taking him into his arms and weeping with joy,
or the only word of his I still recall: sword.
Even the joy of Anna, who was famous as far as Nazareth,
gave little comfort.

A dozen years later,
on our way home from Jerusalem,
we feared the worst when he went missing.
We thought slavers had carried him to Cappadocia or Egypt,
or robbers had killed him for sport.
For three nights and days we chased
the smallest stories to empty ends
until we heard someone mention the temple
and a remarkable boy who asked too many questions.
We knew, without knowing, that we had found him.
In the door, we paused to breathe
for the first time to breathe
our hearts disbelieving the truth:
that our son was beyond anything we could teach,
any rule we could devise,
any rebuke we could force from our hearts.
Our job was simply this:
Under and over the suffering,
to trust, to witness and to love.

II. The Prelude

John

I was a wild child
with parents too old to know what to do
when I wandered the hills for days at a time.
They imagined me fasting, praying,
giving thanks to God for the gift of my life.
Instead, I spied on the Samaritan women
by the Jordan washing their legs;
I tortured the locusts I caught,
threw rocks at the priests, feeling on fire
with rage at something I could not name
until the day I walked through a slot canyon
and the rains stormed themselves into a torrent
that poured around my legs, then chest,
while I clung to a rock, my head under water at times
as I struggled for clean air that finally came,
filling my lungs with sun that felt like song.
Now it was my turn to go to the Jordan,
stare at my reflection, see my sins and the sins of others.
I knew the viper in me and others and called it by name:
the demons that snake their way through our veins.
I washed myself once again, not in salt or sand,
but in flowing water. When a traveler saw me,
I looked up, called him a sinner, invited him to join me.
He did, and I held him under for a moment.
He rose from the water in disbelief
and belief, shocked by the cold truth of his goodness.
He called others to come, and they did.
More followed, including one whom I had not seen in years.
He came into the water, bringing with him
the weight of his desire, a white fire of hope;
I did what he told me and heard the voice
That seemed to include me in its claim and praise.

All this gave me courage to call Herod to task.
He dragged me away to where I belonged:
in the prison of his company, preaching to the one
who could do the most good, who needed the most love
and the courage to trust the water and the sun.

Jesus at the Jordan

I hadn't expected the voice to be so clear.
The only sound I heard at first,
with my head held under water,
was the rush of the current in my veins.
I could see only the dark and the light
swirling together in the mottled water.
When I emerged, I heard the words confirming
What I had suspected, feared,
trusted and doubted all my life.
In an instant, I knew
but had yet to understand.

I traded river for desert, water for sand
outside Jericho, feeling as if I needed to pray
to the one who called me son.
At first, I met only the devils of boredom and loneliness.
Then the Torah returned to me.
I recalled the prophecies
until they were as familiar to me as the ants and wasps
of the hard rock on which I prayed.
I grew hungrier with each passing day,
including the day I realized Elijah and Isaiah
were writing about me. I saw my story unfold,
knew that it would end with death and more.
That's when the Devil came, making me hungry
for the manna with which Yahweh once blessed us,
then for significance, thinking I could unite all kings,
all peoples, for all time, forcing upon them
a yoke of peace. Then I hungered for life
beyond life, to rush to the end of my story.
I faced these doubts, these fears and desires,
and they fled. I felt light with hunger and purpose
and left the desert for the synagogue,
remembering the night sky filled with signs
reminding me who I was and who I am.
I knew I had to tell the truth to any who would listen

and believe, who would learn to hear the voice
that spoke to me past the waters and sands and sky
Telling me, telling us all, that we are loved
and that after the darkness would be wondrous life.

III. In Galilee

The First Friend

I first saw him when we were boys,
barely four, playing outside the synagogue,
and then studying for our bar mitzvah,
celebrating when we became men together.
He drew me to him—the force of his eyes,
the way he listened when I spoke
and heard what I tried to say beyond my words.
When he walked to the Jordan to hear John,
I followed. I didn't know it then,
but my world turned on that instant.
I saw him rise from the waters dripping like a newborn,
the sunlight dancing on his brown skin.
When we returned to Nazareth, he made straight for the synagogue.
I sat on a bench that he had made with his father,
where he and I long ago sat to listen
to the rabbi read from the scroll,
its words filled with fire and iron.
Now he walked to the altar, unrolled the text and read.
I heard, for the first time, the language of God.

The old men did not like what they heard—
that they would be left behind.
They dragged him to the hill above the synagogue
and made to throw him over the edge.
When he turned and faced them,
they saw what I saw, and he walked through them
and away from his home.

Once again, I followed, yelling to my brother as I left
to tell my wife and children
that I would be back later, but not tonight.

We walked, a handful of us,
only knowing that we had no home,
only the road to Capernum.
When we entered the synagogue there,

a man raved and thrashed, hurling curses,
returning stare for stare.
The darkness in the madman saw the light
and fled, shouting new names for my friend.
Messiah. Emmanuel. Savior.

I think that's when he knew beyond all doubt
that the voice above the Jordan was not a dream.
When he saw the woman with the fever,
he ordered it out as if it were a demon. And it fled.
We few followers barely believed what we saw.
But the people of Capernaum lined the streets
waiting their turn for his hands to land on them
and cure hemorrhoids, tumors and sadness of soul.

I stood in line, too, asking for his hands to heal
and forgive the wound I knew I would leave,
back at home, where my wife and child waited,
never understanding, perhaps, what I feel called to do,
And who, now, I feel called to love.

Peter

All night long we flung our nets onto the dark water,
pulling in only two small fish,
not even a breakfast for the three of us.
We had borrowed money to buy this boat.
We feared we might never pay it off. Then, when dawn came,
we rowed to shore where a crowd on the beach
listened to a man we had never seen before.
We hopped over the side and yanked the boat to our mooring.
He stepped in and asked us to row him out a bit.
We could have cared less about this man,
our backs on fire from the night's work,
but curiosity got the better of us.
Sitting there, listening to him,
I started laughing at his hard nonsense.
It's no more possible for me to forgive an enemy
than to lend him more than he desired.
My desire was to go home, lay down, have my wife
rub my neck and shoulders and repair the nets while I slept.
So when he asked me to row out again for more fishing,
I was ready to throw him into the water.
I didn't. Again, curious, amused, we rowed.
When he told us to throw out our nets, we did.
Then the sea itself began to writhe, alive with fins and tails,
fish fighting to leap into nets we thought would break from the weight.
We struggled to bring them in and yelled at our cousins to come
and help with this catch that spilled onto the planks
and piled almost to the oarlocks.
We rowed the best we could
with this swirling mass of scaly flesh dancing all around us.
I knew we could pay our debt and more; stories would be told
for years about this haul, and, I realized, about this man
sitting still in the boat watching me the whole time.
When we finally dragged the boat on shore, he took me aside
and told me to leave everything: the fish and money,
the fame and stories, my children and wife, and follow him.
My partners heard too. We looked at each other,

still giddy, smelling of fish, laughing at ourselves
as we said yes and walked away from what we knew
towards a world, we imagined, where each day
would hold a new miracle.

The Leper

After my marriage and two children,
the blotches appeared,
black scabs on my forehead and hands.
I had to flee to the caves just outside town
where others had gone. The unclean.
We made a family there. Some I had known
back when their skin had shone like sunlight.
We still had wives, husbands, cousins, parents
who left us food. They still loved us,
though we stopped loving ourselves,
wondering what we had done to deserve this curse.
My new family and I shared this:
our loathing of our flesh, always in motion, decaying,
falling away to be buried before the death of our head and heart.
This slow dying was too much, and when I heard the news
that seemed too good and too true,
I brought shame to my family once again
by returning to my town, walking past the shouts
and stones thrown by children
until I stood before the man I had come to challenge,
by daring him to heal me, begging him
to make me love myself again.
He walked to me, embraced me,
kissed my blackened skin, which fell away
like scales scraped from a fish, revealing new flesh.
The price for this, he told me, was death
of a bird and a goat, the sacrifice Moses demanded,
the levy that would lead me back to my family,
back to myself, like a newborn worthy of love.

The Paralytic

We five were friends since childhood,
each born only days apart, growing up together,
marrying, learning our fathers' trades.
I was stonecutter, and a home I built
broke me when a loose block fell
on the small of my back, freezing my legs.
My friends never left. They cared for my wife and child.
They brought wine and dice and tried to draw
the laughter from me they knew I still held.
But that part was frozen too.
I yelled at my family. I cursed my friends for still coming.
I stopped praying, except to curse God.
When my friends told me the stories they had heard,
a healer with the heart of the sky,
I wanted no part of it. They carried me anyway,
half-a-day's walk to the next town,
where thick crowds blocked the one badly built hall.
I could see it was poorly made. Even pointed out the loose tiles
on the roof to my pallbearers. (That's what I called these men.)
They smiled when I told them this and carried me to the hillside
behind the room and then onto the roof.
Two of them pried the tiles loose.
The other two jumped down.
Still tied to my bed,
I was handed from roof to floor
when all noise stopped, and he looked at my broken back
and saw pain, fear, hatred, rage,
and the self-pitying fool I had become.
He made me see myself. Then he forgave me
for stilling my heart all these years.
I wept when he told me to stand, to carry my bed,
to leave and start living again and see myself for who I was:
a man loved, still able to love, able to walk now
and then run, all the way home
to ask my family for forgiveness.

The Levi

I had heard the story of the leper; rather,
I overheard it. Few people back then
ever spoke directly to me. I was the leper,
a man, they believed, who took more than his due.
True, sometimes I did,
but only from those whose stones and curses
I felt at my back when I passed them in the streets.
Maybe that's why I leapt up when he came early,
just at dawn, outside my home,
the sky firing the clouds to a golden rose.
That's all it took: a kind word or two,
an invitation for friendship, even more.
The hard words did not stop that night
at supper surrounded by the only friends I had:
others like myself, sons of tax collectors,
destined, like sons of butchers or undertakers,
to do the work that stained our hands
with blood or money. But around him,
my hands felt useful, clean, and kind.
His hand brushed mine at dinner when he passed the bread;
even then I heard the mutterings outside,
wondering how he could be seen with me,
let alone share a meal.
That's when I fell in love …
I have no other words for what I felt
when he spoke his riddle about wine skins.
It took the priests a moment to understand, and when they did,
their faces turned crimson, colored deeper than morning clouds,
the blood of shame rushing, I like to think,
reminding them of their cruelty to me,
reminding me, as well, of my meanness.
That flash of sorrow was the tax on my soul,
the price I paid to stay with him three years,
even after he left,
when returning to my old ways made no sense.
The only thing that mattered

was the brush of his hand, the kind word,
and the embrace of dawn
calling me each day to life.

Andrew

This was the day he drew lines.
We started early one morning,
the sun hot on our shoulders as we cut through a wheat field;
even the Pharisees came, some still hoping he would be on their side,
some wanting to catch him in the act this Sabbath.
All of us felt hungry. We watched
as he picked a grain of wheat,
threshed it with his hands, rubbing away the shell,
then eating the kernel raw. We did the same
making a breakfast of grain and laughter
as we heard the Pharisees' bitter prattle
of empty condemnation.
This was the first line we crossed.
Later, when he cured a man's withered hand,
I felt my own calloused hands and heart cleansed of my sins.
But the Scribes abandoned him, siding with the Pharisees,
deciding that he must be stopped.
They debated just how to do so
in their cold tangle of logic and scripture.

He spent the night in prayer alone,
as he sometimes did, atop a hill
with no company except stars and angels.
When he came down in the morning,
he looked on fire with the dawn,
lines of light behind him,
seeming to come from his head, hands and feet.
That's when he drew lines, linking us,
calling the 12, speaking my name,
telling me on what side I would forever stand:
with those who choose love,
who follow only one line, one rule, one way:
Love beyond all measure, as if love were a wind,
impelling me towards myself.

III. IN GALILEE

That day, standing there, called to love by this man,
I felt I was my best self,
desiring to be that way forever.

The Apostate

At first I was drawn to his words of being blessed
and being loved, but when he spoke of sharing cloaks,
turning cheeks, loving enemies, being hungry,
I walked away. I sat on the hillside watching him
as he continued to preach to these sheep-like men,
who listened without thinking to the import of his words.
When he spoke about homes with no foundation, he looked my way.
I could bear it no longer.
I walked away, knowing that my life was good enough.
I was content knowing
who my enemies were and would always be,
that food and joy would always bless my home
and not the hunger and sorrow of which he spoke.
The further I walked, the more sure I became
of my familiar answers, the old ways,
the trust I had that love alone would not sustain me.
Only me and my answers—not the questions
that, from time to time, still haunt me.

The Centurion

I came to Galilee a hard man, hired by Herod
to lead my 80 men across Meshech and Tubal
to this place by the lake.
It made me soft, I think, living here
with nothing to do but keep my men battle-ready
and their hands off the girls and women.
One worked for me, a woman with a young son;
he became my servant. I grew to love him
as if he were my own. I imagined some of my men
whispered that I was buggering him,
but I could not imagine harm coming his way.
He made me fond of his tribe, just as I had grown fond
of my tribe of soldiers, these men and boys
far from the hillsides of their homes.
I even built a synagogue in town,
Something to keep my men occupied, to remind them
that we were builders as well as warriors.
The favor of the Jews saved me
when the boy grew limp with fever.
They told me about a healer,
and I dispatched the rabbi to ask this holy man,
this messenger of God, to come to my home.
Within an hour, my misgivings overtook me,
and I sent another to beg him to cast his spell
from afar. I was afraid he would see in me
too much of my own past battles,
the blood that spilled from my dreams.
I was not worthy of his presence and blessing.
When the boy rose from his bed,
ran outside, and pretended to be a centurion
issuing orders at my men, I wept,
believing beyond my unbelief,
that there was still goodness left in me
that someone else could see, even miles away.

The Widow

My son was not merely my son.
My neighbors also called him their own.
When he ran through the alleys as a boy,
he led a line of children trailing behind
who tried to catch his shadow
and climb the stones he had climbed.
Even after his father had died, I smiled often,
delighting in the laughter and light that filled our home
simply because he was my son.
He was so unlike my husband and me.
We both wondered what angel
had brought him to us as alive as a firefly.
Then, when fever boiled his whole body,
shaking him with spasms of fire and water,
I shook with him, dreading the end I suspected.
When death came, I almost felt relieved;
I could finally stop fearing his death
and the dying that would soon embrace me.
My cousins put his body, wrapped tight with linen and spices,
atop the bier the day he died.
The cloth hid the light still glowing in his skin.
When this stranger came,
leading his own line of trailing men,
I felt only anger at his intrusion on my grief
And the attention paid someone other than my son
Or me. He stopped. He saw my ragged face.
He touched my son's bier and body.
Some whispered the word "defile."
But I heard the words he whispered,
and my heart stirred when my son's arm
raised itself, as if to greet the new day.
I did not know what to think.
I had almost found a new home in my solitude and tears,
in the hollow where my heart had been.
As my son stood, unbound,
smelling still of sweet death,

III. In Galilee

I fell to my knees. In fear. In joy.
In glory. In disbelief, daring myself
To believe that this was real,
laughing along with my laughing son,
and weeping as he wept.

The Wanton

Before my wedding day, my mother gave me
an alabaster jar filled with oil and spice
to anoint my husband before we lay together.
He did not want to wait, but took me
as he would a farm animal, beating me
for good measure, he said, to teach me my place
in his house. I left soon after,
refusing to live in his world, under his fist.
I took up with one man after another,
men who used me according to their will.
I let them, as I saw no good in me worth guarding.
I could find no work other than gleaning the harvest.
When I heard about the man they called the Messiah,
I wondered, as did everyone, who he was:
a zealot and lunatic
or a messenger of the almighty
who could taste the bitterness of my shadow.
Even John sent emissaries, as did the Pharisees
who invited him to supper. Then I remembered the jar
and thought of my wedding night.
I went to find him to anoint him,
hoping that by cleansing him,
I would wash away a portion of the filth that had filled me.
A part of me sought the husband I had once prayed for,
and another part wanted to know this: "Who am I?"
When I bathed his feet, I looked at him
and saw the answer in his eyes.
I was myself again, the young girl who once ran
with the boys in the streets, who sat still
as my mother combed my hair
and my father sang to me.
I was anointed, finally, by his kindness
and by the oil that blessed us both.

Joanna

The stories speak of the 12, but we know better.
We three women who walked stride for stride
with these men and boys. I think we knew better than they
just what this man could do. People speak of Mary's seven demons.
She called them devils for the ache in her head so painful
that she felt as if needles were piercing her eyes.
He held her hands, massaged her wrists, kissed her brow,
and the pain fled, left her as if driven by a wind.
For Susanna, the knot in her stomach untied itself
when he laid his hands on the tumor.
The storytellers have forgotten what he did for my husband,
Chuza, steward to Herod, keeper of all his accounts,
buyer and seller of land, animals, linen and spice.
Chuza grew mean-spirited, on fire with profit and gain.
He whipped his servants, cheated farmers, even tried to beat me once.
That's when I sought help from the Nazarene.
I brought Chuza to him one day, lying to my husband,
telling him about a bargain to be had.
The temptation was too great. When the two met,
Chuza saw something, felt his demons stirring,
saw the seeds of his life's work sown onto hard ground,
saw what bitter and foreign weeds had taken root in his heart.
"Sin no more," was all Chuza had to hear
to return to himself, to the man whom I once knew
to be generous, gentle and patient.
That's when my husband asked me
to join this family of Galileans, to walk with them
from town to village, to pay for what was needed
with money that needed redemption
in thanks for a heart redeemed, the two of us ourselves again,
like seeds finally growing in rich soil,
coming into full flower.

James, Jesus' brother

He was eight years my senior, and the two of us
Cared for our mother after our father had died.
I remember him smiling and laughing in our youth.
He taught me so much about animals,
birds, flowers, trees, the small changes
brought by each season. He told me to pay attention
to the variations in feathers, seed heads, clouds,
to see more than what I first found, to see beyond this world.
He was a good teacher. Then he left, telling me to care for Mary.
All she did was worry, as mothers do.
One day, when he was nearby, she insisted we see him.
We walked for two days, eating only cheese
and hard bread dipped in olive oil.
When we saw the crowds, we knew he stood at their center.
Word came to him that we had arrived. Word came back to us
that he would not see us. He made a point to all who would hear
that his family went beyond blood.
Mother didn't care about such lessons. She pushed her way in,
dragging me along. I was embarrassed to be led, at my age, by the hand.
Then he saw us, smiled, and embraced us both
leaving me feeling envy, shame, anger
and then love of what I was witnessing:
a change greater than that of the seasons,
larger, I suspected, than even my brother knew,
as these crowds cheered and pressed closer,
looking for the same embrace that claimed them as family.

III. In Galilee

Bartholomew

I must have suffered death by water once before;
it haunts my dreams: I fall from a boat into blackness,
unable to kick to the surface, weighed down by sodden clothes
and sins I barely recall. That's why, I think,
when the water sloshed into the boat,
kicked up by a southern squall, I panicked
and put a scare into the others. Andrew started bailing water,
but I rushed to the master on the other end of this bucking boat,
its one mast shivering and shaking like my heart.
I shook the rabbi, who woke. With one look,
he saw my fear and made me feel foolish
with his calm certitude. The others were shouting orders
at each other; then, as he stood, they told him to stay low.
He ignored them, turned to the wind, sucked in as much air
as his lungs could hold, and shouted: "Enough!"
to the seas and sky. Within seven of my breaths, black clouds
opened to azure and the whitecaps sank to indigo.
Some of us kept our hands on the buckets, bailing more slowly.
We all watched the skies to see if the storm would dare return.
Then he sat down, finally, looked at us and smiled,
wondering, perhaps, what we were wondering
as we sat on our wet benches, unsure of what we all had seen
and what we all knew:
that this man could speak to the winds and waves
just as he spoke to my heart, telling me:
enough. End my fear of death, which now seemed to me
a door to someplace new and solid,
not a watery and black descent to uncertainty.

The Demoniac

I speak now with one voice,
move in one straight line,
the author of my life, choosing my words and ways.
I can't recall when the demons came
pouring into me like a swarm of bees.
I'm told that I was 19 when so many voices
crowded my skull that I felt only the heat
of confusion and tore off my clothes.
That day, I ran to the lake, to the hills,
to a small grove of trees where the voices in my skull
spoke to some other sound not of this earth
that came up through the holes in the ground
that moved their soiled lips in reply to the babble in my brain.
At times, my friends and cousins would find me,
tie me with chains, but I knew how to cut myself
and make my skin slick with blood,
to wrestle my ankles free and race to the stone tombs
where I saw the spirits that had not yet found their way
from life to death.
They lingered with me and howled back at the demons,
each tormenting the other.
That all changed the day he arrived.
The demons in me sensed him coming, knew his name,
made me call it out in fear
that they would go the way of smoke and ash, not even to Gehenna.
He spoke their name: Legion. They asked him
to cast them into the pigs that we raise to trade
with the Gentiles. These animals that eat their own filth
and that can chew off the leg of a stumbling swineherd
were the only fit hosts for these unclean demons.
They left me with a spasm so violent that I thought I might fly with them
and leap into the lake for death by water and mud.
Instead, I returned to a silence I had not heard in years.
I broke it myself when I thanked this man, who gave me his cloak
to hide my blackened body. By now a crowd surrounded us.
They were so used to me crazed

that they railed against this change and the loss of their livestock.
I think they feared other cast-out demons might find new homes
in their panicked brains. When I asked to sail with these men,
he told me no and asked me this, simply this:
to tell what happened, and I did, for the rest of my days,
even when people stopped believing me,
I told the story, this story, about the author of life.

Ruth

I was the bleeder. That is how people knew me.
I was the one whose time of the month
lasted the entire month, every year since I had turned 12.
I announced myself with the stink of all that stained me.
At first, the physicians tried yarrow to staunch the flow.
When that failed, we made sacrifices at the temple:
small birds whose blood would redeem the sins
my parents assumed I had committed, too much touching
or vile thoughts or a curse from an aggrieved neighbor.
They began hitting me for no reason other than this:
to convince themselves that the blame lay in me,
not them, not God, not the natural order of life.
For years I had endured,
so when I first heard of this healer,
I dared myself to believe
or resign myself to a life that stank like death.
When he stepped off the boat,
the crowds swallowed him whole,
pushing him toward Jairus' house and daughter.
I struggled through, my way made easier
when two neighbors saw me. They parted,
like the red sea that I had become,
disgusted and fearful that I might touch them.
When I slipped past the crowd and grew close to the Nazarene,
I thrust my arm toward him, grazed his cloak,
and froze as he turned to me, asking his question:
"Who?" I collapsed, feeling for the first time
something strange not stirring in me, a wholeness
that frightened me with its newness.
He bent to me, put his face close to mine,
and thanked me for my faith, for being more
than a creature of blood and flesh, for knowing
that the only sin would have been to let this moment
pour out, like a final drop of blood.

Jairus' Daughter

At 12, I suffered a fever more red
and intense than any that had ever fired me before.
I lay in bed drenched and kicking,
Imagining my room moving, each wall
alive with the desire to close in on me.
And then they did, and I died,
I think, seeing nothing except my life
as it had been these dozen years or so.
Even I wasn't sure how many nights
I had slept or how long I would sleep now
that my light had shifted out of my body
to this new place, where silence overtook me.
I felt buried in peace and saw what would happen next:
The roots entering my tomb, seeking food from my flesh,
my bones sprouting new limbs, green and alive
that would rise to the light and dance in the wind.
I felt a calmness beyond understanding.
Then I heard my name being called: Chava.
Come back to life. And I obeyed, pouring myself
through my branches, back into my roots,
up into my bones. I opened my eyes,
as if for the first time, and saw the disbelief
that had been in my parents' faces before,
and their unbelief at seeing me now,
alive, craving berries, honey, cheese and dates,
and a few more days yet to dance
on this side of the divide.

James

He sent us empty-handed on the road in a dozen directions
telling us to heal, to cast out demons,
to learn who we were and what we could do
as ambassadors of a man we were just getting to know.
On the road to Tiberias, I paused to speak
to a young boy selling melons from a cart.
He tried to bargain with me, but I only laughed,
repeating that I had no money. He relented
and took me by my hand to his home, a small hut,
unfinished, on the fringe of the city.
His mother, I saw, suffered from gout, his father,
from poor vision. I asked to touch them both,
whispering prayers that we had overheard,
not secret incantations, simply blessings,
thanking the creator for life and breath.
When they saw each other healed,
they ran to tell their neighbors. Even the priest,
dressed in his best robes, came. Some wanted healing,
others begged me to stay with them in their homes,
larger, more elegant, filled with rugs, oil lamps
and sweet foods. I declined, but worked
to help those I could, praying with my hands
over the open wounds, deaf ears and lame limbs
of these men and women torn by accidents
and their own dissolute living.
These latter I challenged, like the master did, to sin no more.
When I left, I carried with me one gift:
a melon the boy gave me. I ate it on the way back,
each slice a smile, a reminder that these good people
taught me what I could do once I realized
that I was an echo of someone else,
of something even greater yet to come.

Herod

I was anxious to see this man
whom some were saying was John the Baptist
come back to life, his head
no longer severed from his neck.
This man cured the sick and raised the dead.
Had he returned for revenge?
Should I have been frightened? I felt nothing
save curiosity, and, if I'm honest with myself,
a little hope for conversation,
something to fill the empty spaces in the day.
I loved debating the hermit.
I looked forward to our dungeon conversations
more than my time in Rome,
more than my brother's wife, now my own,
or even her dancing daughter.
He could do something no one else could:
Make me wonder sometimes
how God's laws applied even to a tetrarch.
He helped me forget my jealousies,
my resentment at my enemies,
my regret at battles lost by bad advice.
So I wanted to see this new healer,
to meet someone walking through my door
who had something amusing to say,
and who, like John, would also make me forget
the sadness that buzzes about me,
like flies around a head.

Judas

Why is it I always feel the loneliest in crowds?
We were 5,000 gathered on a meadow by the sea,
a mile from town, and all I wanted
was to be alone with him,
to receive the blessing of his touch and gaze.
Instead, he left us with a problem: how to feed 5,000.
I felt I was the leader of the 12. Older than most,
smarter than Peter, I talked the others into this plan:
Send the crowd away. But the master wouldn't listen.
He asked us to have them sit in cohorts of fifty,
to wait patiently for food to come like manna from the ground.
He asked for the food we did have: five loaves of bread; two fish.
He held the basket in his arms, lifted it above his head,
said a blessing for all to hear: "Thank you for what we have,
for what we need; for those who need more, we pray
they are blessed by the gift of this day."
When the basket made its rounds, I watched
as a terrible thing happened.
You're not supposed to get something from nothing;
there's always a price to pay.
When the 5,000 had eaten,
when each of the 12 held a basket of leftovers
almost too heavy to carry, we wondered what had happened.
We had argued over the healings,
even the stilling of the waters.
Those could be explained away with effort.
This was different. This had no reason behind it.
And when I thought of my own father,
bent from years of hunger, I burned a bit,
questioning this man whom I loved,
who made his own rules in his own time.
When, I wondered, would the payback come.

John the younger

I was always the first to find him
when he went off to pray.
I couldn't bear being out of his sight for too long,
away from the light he inspired within me;
he made me feel whole, at peace,
aware of who I was
and grateful to the God who made me this way.
When I found him, I called to the others.
He sat on a stone in the dappled shade of a few pines,
their needles knitting the sunlight.
He looked the way I wanted to feel,
his hands resting on his thighs,
palms upright, eyes staring ahead at nothing,
at everything. When the others arrived,
he asked us about the crowds
and what they said of him.
We often mingled with the villagers and shepherds.
Some called him John or Elijah returned on his chariot.
He asked us what we thought.
I said nothing. I didn't need him to be anything
other than what he was: my teacher, my friend,
my sign that God was here, alive and kind.
Peter didn't wait too long to answer:
"You are the Messiah."
Then Jesus smiled at this fisherman, this bull of a man,
and asked us not to repeat the name
we suddenly knew was true.

Then he asked us to close our eyes.
He showed each of us our own death.
This was his dark gift to us.
Later, when we shared those visions,
We all agreed that we no longer feared dying,
even by stone or sword.
Most of us forgot this the day the crowds tried to find us,
to drag us to the foot of his cross and stone us.

But at that place among the pines,
we knew that the life after this one was better,
that the souls we carried like babies,
would be born anew if we kept faith,
if we believed in this man,
if we gave ourselves over to the call
to sit with him in prayer, breathing in words
that helped us to see a world on fire with light.

Jesus on Tabor

In the early morning,
before the boulders blazed with heat,
we left the desert floor
for the mountain
to the place where God's mind danced:
A cowl and cave that called to me.
I brought with me three of the twelve:
my heart, my head and my hands—
one who loved me as I love God,
one who thought about each step he took,
and one who leapt into action before thinking.
We tied our clothing around our waist
and climbed on boulders and cliffs,
scraping our shins against the edges of the sky
until we stopped to rest. Then the light erupted
with an apparition of Moses, who met God on a mountain,
and Elijah, who heard God at the mouth of a cave.
They showed me the prophecy of my betrayal and torture,
the nails pounded into my wrists,
the thorns biting into my skull,
my end interrupted by a journey
to the center of death, a place colder
than the desert floor in winter.
I was, for a moment, what I would become:
Light shining with light, love turning inward
and beyond, an eye, a hand, a heart,
seeing beyond the end of time,
when each molecule would return to the source,
shards and fragments of selves merging and reforming
into wondrous shapes, times and places beyond understanding.
Then I heard his voice again,
speaking not to me, but to my friends,
telling them the simple truth: that I was the chosen son,
and they should listen, just as Elijah had
to the stillness and whisper of God
hidden in what I said, in what I did.

James on Tabor

I did not know where he was leading us,
but I knew to follow, each step deliberate,
sure, looking for stable footholds
as my brother and Peter leapt after the master,
each stepping in his steps, trusting that he knew the way.
When we finally stopped, we sat, stretched,
then dozed, dreaming the same dream:
Elijah and Moses—how we knew
we will never know—speaking of our Lord's death.
Peter wanted to mark this moment
by building shelters, alcoves, cairns—something
to protect and remember, right here,
on what we knew now was the mountain of God.
Peter barely finished speaking when we entered
the vault of God's mind and heard the words
our hearts had already guessed:
This man we followed from town to town
was the son of God.
We knew then our fate would be his fate
and that we would never again know home
until the day we stood before God
and hear him call us beloved,
just as he did atop Tabor
when the wind and birds stilled themselves
so that we could listen to the whispered voice
hiding in our hearts.

The Epileptic's Father

I never believed the stories of possession;
he was my son and not even I possessed him.
He was his own until the shaking
knocked him to the ground
sending his eyes into his head
to see visions he could never remember.
Those who said a devil sat inside his skull
saw every blemish as a mark of weakness and sin.
But he was my son, my beloved,
and when the healer came, I brought him forward.
It was too much. He convulsed, screwing himself
into the dust at the feet of the master,
who knelt and held his head between his hands
just for a moment, long enough to heal.
When my son's eyes returned to the light,
he rose, embraced this man, and told the village
the good news of what he had seen in his trance,
a vision he could now recall—the end of days
on a green plain, a meadow where we would be
before long, singing psalms of praise
in new voices to the one sky.

Philip

I know I wasn't the greatest,
but listened at night to those who sided with Peter
and to those who favored James.
Even John, the youth, had his faction
that took note of his ascent of Tabor
and his silence when he returned.
I wondered why no one had mentioned me.
I felt a hollowness when my thoughts turned to this dark place,
to the fear that others ranked me last.
That darkness sat in me even when the master
gathered us by the well
and placed a child on his knee.
He sensed my envy and jealousy:
mirrors to each other,
pride staring back at self-loathing.
He told us all to be small like a child,
like a porter, a builder as he had been born,
a farmer worrying about rent, taxes and rain.
Be like them, he said,
not like the priests, the Romans,
the hangers-on in Herod's palace.
Be like them and rank and wealth
will not plague your life.
He told us he would die poor and shamed
and to be like him.
I'm not sure why, but this lifted the darkness,
made me spit it out
like a bone that had been stuck in my throat,
and I rested easy in the place I held,
which was no place at all,
a position as impervious as the air.

Mark

He said so much that I wanted to recall,
each phrase a poem, a psalm
beyond David's strumming.
I committed them to memory
just as I had committed myself to his cause.
The least is the greatest.
Anyone not against you is for you.
The foxes have holes, birds have nests,
but I have nowhere to lay my head.
Leave the dead to bury the dead.
Once your hand is on the plough, never look back.
I would take one of these and pray with it
as I walked, each word conjuring a world
of images, stories, truths
from my life as a child and bearded youth.
These sayings became my companions and guides,
teaching me new lessons with each sunlit day,
surprising me with new rooms of meaning,
new ways of seeing my twisted life.
They untangled me, let me see everything
as prelude to this time,
this man, these truths
that I will tell to anyone
willing to listen
and brave enough to believe.

IV. The Journey

One of the 72

I felt called to a new force,
not so much an army of Maccabees
but a new priesthood, men whom he trusted
to trust the world, to walk among the towns
without fear of bandit attack,
the slip of a dagger across our throats
or pushed past our ribs.
I put these thoughts aside
and arrived in villages toward dusk,
the dust of the road still on me,
and began speaking.
Without fail, men would form a circle
thinking me crazy at first, wondering
what cult of a crazed messiah I represented.
When I named the Nazarene as my master,
they stopped talking, listened harder,
took me in and fed me,
wanted to know if he planned to come himself
and heal their mothers, wives and sons
as they heard he had done elsewhere.
They asked me what he meant
when I repeated his stories.
They wondered when blood would spill
and what burdens he would lift from their backs:
taxes, rent, raids or Roman rule.
When I left, they gave me food.
When the 72 regrouped with the master and the 12,
we marveled at the stories we heard echoed by us all:
Satan fell from the sky like lightning
wherever we went, and light shined
in the faces of those we met.
Then we danced and sang, unable to contain our joy
that we had cured, that we had been called,
that we belonged to him.

The Lawyer

Before I came to love God,
I learned to hate him.
From the moment I was born,
my father named me part of his tribe:
I was a scribe, destined to know the law,
copy the Torah, arrange contracts—
work, I found, that ground me into dust
as I watched those my age
labor in the fields with their fathers,
their hands caked clean with mud.
I stayed inside, copying the Torah on animal skins,
following the strictures of 48 and 60 letters per line,
mixing my own ink, speaking each word
as I wrote it, washing myself
before writing the sacred name of YHVH—
I took more pleasure in composing my own psalms,
imagining I had David's lyre and tongue,
whenever I saw a new blue leaf
beside a white blossom blessed with sunlight and bee-song.
My father would beat me when he saw me
scribbling these songs, even on blemished skins.
He taught me to hate him, to hate myself
and the God who inscribed the wrong title on my life.
The hate with which I clothed myself
could not silence the psalms that sang to me
each morning and night with the long slants
of darkness and light that twined like vines.
When my brother scribes heard of this Messiah
and the return of his 72, they thought of a way to trap him,
and sent me to their gathering place.
They even gave me the question to ask—
one our rabbis had debated in the synagogues and streets—
the question with no right answer,
or so I thought, until I heard it
coming from my own mouth
as if for the first time: two old lines,

one from Deuteronomy, one from Leviticus,
lines that twined like the sunlight,
forming a psalm of their own:
Love your God and your neighbor. Even yourself.
When he affirmed their truth,
I felt free to love and forgive myself, my father, my God,
to inscribe on my heart the one word
that names me, that made me clean,
that sings through me to this day.

Lawyer II: Parable.

When I asked him a question—
What is the greatest commandment?—
He replied by asking me, "What do *you* say?"
So when he praised my answer
I replied with a question:
Who is my neighbor?
Then he wove a story
about a bandit, some zealot
laying in wait behind a hillock,
taking his dagger out from a fold in his cloak
and stabbing a traveler, leaving him to bleed
in the ditch by the road.
Both a priest and Levite pass him by,
as I might, thinking the man besotted,
mad or crawling with lice.
But a third man stops,
takes time to turn him, to see the wound
like a mouth still whispering pulses of blood.
He rips his own cloak to bandage him,
washes the wound with oil and water,
embraces him from behind, arms under arms,
to hoist him up and onto his donkey,
leading both man and animal into Jericho,
where the sun beats the road into rock
and even the shade burns to the touch.
He places him in an inn, pays for his care and keep,
offers to return with more money.
And then the parable ends with a question:
Who proved himself a neighbor?
I answered without speaking the name of our enemy.
I was still playing the lawyer, the scribe who spoke
just enough. I had learned my trade too well
to follow this man with all my
heart, soul, strength and mind.
But his question buried itself in me
like some insect or mole, and I knew

IV. The Journey

I would spend the rest of my life
feeling that question dig its way out:
How much was I willing to risk
to love the world as if she were my bride?

Martha and Mary

Martha: We sniped at each other like only sisters can,
though we didn't start this way.

Mary: We loved being together when we were young,
each insisting that we be alike in everything,
falling asleep at the same time,
learning the words to the same songs,
dancing the same steps as we sang.

Martha: Then we began to resent the other,
denying who we were in our urge to be one.
I was happiest only when I did two jobs at once,
thinking of the other dozen jobs left to do.

Mary: I could not stand my sister's labors, her belief
that running through the house reminding me of my work
was the only way to be. I simply wanted to *be*,
to sit by the fire and watch the embers grow golden,
fly into the air and light the night sky.
I wanted to enjoy each visitor we had,
let the conversation carry me to someplace new.

Martha: I blamed my sister for her not seeing
the 10 things we needed to do before each meal,
the dozen that had to be done after we ate.
She left me all the work and feeling righteous
in my anger and resentment.
But never hate. And that's what saved us
as old women, when we lived with each other
and with what we had suffered.

Mary: It came to a head the first time we met the Master.
I had heard so much of him. I wanted to hear him for myself
and see this man some called the Messiah.

IV. The Journey

Martha: I wanted to impress him with my cooking,
the cleanliness of our home, have him compliment me
on how hard I worked and how much I managed to do
in so short a time. Even Lazarus ...

Mary: ... Lazarus laughed at us, each trying too hard
to win his affection, to prove ourselves the favorite.
And that also held us together, how much
we both loved our brother, younger than us,
in our charge after our mother's death.

Martha: Later, much later, we saw just how much
the Master loved him too, and we sounded
the depth of his love, which echoed in the work I did
and in my sister's quiet study
of this man whose stay proved too brief,
who left us bereft and blessed.

Thomas

I envied him, the look that would come
to him as he prayed.
He would sit, breathe, wrestle with his worries,
set them to the side, breathe again,
and open his eyes to something new:
a certain place, where he saw beyond
anything I could see or hear or touch.
When he rose one day, I asked him:
Teach me to pray, and he threw words into the air
like strands of rope, connecting,
encircling, braiding with the divine,
even with the woman who shouted out that his mother was blessed:
He encircled her within the arc of his love,
as he did the Pharisee who invited him to eat,
as he did the man possessed by the mute demon.
I wonder now: If the demon who fled the silent man could speak,
would he not plead to enter the circle
where we twelve lived in the embrace of this man,
who taught us that praying meant more than chanting words
or washing hands before sitting for dinner?

The Hateful Brother

All I asked was a simple question:
May I have my share of the inheritance?
My father gave nearly all to my older brother,
though he had promised me a fair division.
I know how the world works.
My friends look at how I dress,
where I eat, how generous I am at the inn,
and measure me accordingly.
I am poorer than I should be.
I spend my nights crying to my wife
and cursing the God and my father
who halved me of my good name.

Then this son of man came to town
with a reputation as a healer.
I brought to him my wound,
the wrong done to me,
my heart bleeding like an open sore,
and he used my few words
as an excuse to launch into a lecture
against the dangers of avarice,
the need for simplicity,
the coming storm of war,
the need to prepare for death
with his claim that everlasting treasure
lies beyond this life where neither moth nor thief
can diminish your worth and wealth.

These words stung me more than my father's writ,
more than the darkness of my brother's eyes.
I went home, slept and woke,
thinking about why I worried over
the bitter fruit that hung from the branch of my heart.
From that morning on, I learned to love the ravens
that danced around my garden, eating seeds and beetles,
their black feathers shining blue in the sunlight,

calling to each other as a family would,
with care, with questions, with caution,
before deciding to leave my garden
for their home in the dome of the sky.

The Broken Woman

I was 15 when I lifted the vase
overfull with olive oil that spilled down the sides,
making it hard to grip and staining my clothes.
Then I heard my back snap like a crack in a branch.
Since then, my life has been circumscribed
by a world measured from the knees down.
I knew the insects and seedlings
better than I knew the faces of my family
or past friends, the ones who avoided me,
calling me cursed by God,
not wanting to believe their backs would break
from the strain of a heavy load.
When I was much older, a man came to town
and into the synagogue on the Sabbath.
He told me to stand up straight.
I did just as he asked. The first face I saw was his,
a man neither young nor old,
whose eyes were tired and alive;
he looked at me with no pity—
only compassion, as if we had been childhood friends.
His face told me what I already knew:
With new sight will come new challenges.
Now I need to look people in the face
as they look into my own,
both searching for truth, for meaning, for love,
for the secrets that we hide from ourselves,
the answers that come only when I look at the sky
and it looks back into the darkness of my eyes.

The Synagogue's President

This holy place is my home
just as much as the place where I sleep
and eat and sing to my children.
My kinsmen chose me, holding me up as scrupulous
in following the laws of Moses and the prophets.
I tithed my wages, as well as each spice I added to my meals.
But when this man healed a woman
on the Sabbath, I had to speak up.
It was my duty. If not me, then who?
And for my steadfastness, he called me hypocrite.
His words stung like the stones I thought to throw
to drive him out the door and away from this place.
That night, I knew why his words hurt:
I counted all the times I had lied, cheated, stole,
lusted in my days, even times
I spent the Sabbath for myself, not for God.
My sins stared me down, paraded before me,
revealing me to myself for who I am:
as bent as the women he cured.
I ran after him the next morning to warn him:
Herod is coming for you. Leave.
And pray for me, your servant,
more broken than anyone I know.

The Man with Dropsy

I knew I was bait,
a weever fish brought to the table
to catch a king, a messiah,
a heretic and blasphemer.
My brother, the priest,
brought me to his house
from my home in my swollen self,
my arms like the bladders of a goat
filled with water to bursting,
my skin stretched taut,
my head like an overripe olive,
nothing but pressure and pain
every day, all night.
When I was summoned to the room
where the Pharisees had gathered,
he stared me down, stood up,
came to me, held me close,
and I could feel the water
flow out of my body
into the air perhaps, into the ground,
into some other poor soul.
All I knew is that he freed me
from drowning in my own juices
because he saw me for who I was
and hoped to prove a point:
the laws exist for us,
not the other way around.

Though he sent me away,
I stayed just outside the door
to see if my brother's trap would work.
The master was clever, answering only in story:
But they knew his meaning.
They would never sit at the banquet of heaven.
They lacked the will and the desire
to surrender to what I knew

the moment he touched me.
There is no middle ground,
no going back, only one heart,
one mind, one way forward.

The next day I left with him and the others,
walking to the next town on feet not ready to burst open,
but steady, feeling the soft earth through the soles of my sandals,
my head alive and on fire with a purpose I knew I would soon discover.

Prodigal

I was among those who heard the story
of the son who wanted an early inheritance,
the portion slated for later, and I knew
I was that son, with a thirst nothing could slake,
a desire for all that was denied to me,
the denial fueling my desire
during times of fasting, when hunger led me to eat;
when I was first married, and my neighbor's daughter
had a beauty too soft to ignore.
I was the son who strayed,
who found himself far from home,
far from a law whose lines defined me.

Then I was the father, filled with fear and pity
when my own son left home to see Jerusalem,
eager to see the place where everything
could be bought for enough coins.
He stole from me and left,
but the money meant little compared to the love
that only grew with his leaving.
When my boy returned, I sat with him
at our table and laughed so hard at his tears
that he started laughing too.

Then, when the teacher told of the older brother,
I felt that man's anger that life would never be fair,
and then I was the younger brother
all over again, wanting more than I had,
more than I ever deserved
from a world that offered love
first and sometimes only
in the wildflowers lit by the shafts of dawn.

The Rich Man

I keep clean by keeping the laws.
I do not eat the flesh of swine.
I wash and perfume myself.
I buy cloaks and robes and undergarments
from the best merchants
who import from the best makers
in Alexandria, Damascus, Rome and Sidon.
Of all the Pharisees in this town,
I appreciate quality to a degree
that sets me apart, just as my house
with its marbled floor, bought with the rent
I charge for the land handed to me
by my ancestors, distinguishes me
as a man of wealth and cleanliness.
So when this filthy man that some call a prophet
kicks up the dust of this town onto my purple robe,
I know him for who he is: cursed by the same God
who has blessed me with my wealth.
When he wove his story of Lazarus,
I thought of all the beggars with their sores
that I see each day outside the temple,
in the market, even near my home
searching my trash before my servants burn the mounds
in humble sacrifice and to keep the scum far from me.
I know what brings peace of mind: the best things.
And when my servants fetch me
my packages from Jerusalem, wrapped in cloth,
I feel the anticipation that this time,
I might hold what is worthy of my taste,
and I do, and then that elation fades
to a hollow hunger and thirst that this man with his words
will never satiate nor slake.
He only leaves me wanting more.

The Tenth Leper

Even among us outcasts
there exists a pecking order.
Those with smooth faces hold themselves above the rest.
Those who faces are exposed to the bone, like mine is,
are shunned by our tribe by the caves
where darkness masks us even from ourselves.
The Jews hated me the most,
the only Samaritan in this company of ulcers.
When we heard that the Master would pass near us,
we walked to the roadside and stayed just far enough away
to avoid the rocks of the travelers
but close enough see the crowds
that followed this Son of Man.
When he approached, he knew just by looking
what we needed, and told us to go,
to make ourselves known to the Pharisees,
the men who hated us above all others.
The others grumbled,
wondering if this were a second banishment
or the Master's way of cursing the hypocrites
who made up the priesthood.
Then, when one of my tribe looked down at his hands,
he cried out that he was cured.
We checked our own scars and weeping skin
to see only healthy flesh, muscles and fine hair,
not the purple and black that had marked us as unclean,
the dead only waiting to die.
The others raced to show their families they were whole.
I turned back, praising the one God
who rules Galilee and Samaria,
calling for the Son of Man, finding him;
I threw myself prostrate at his feet,
weeping and seeing him for who he is:
a fellow outcast, hated by the priests,
whose skin would soon be torn and bleeding,
purple and weeping like mine had been
just this morning when death was all I knew.

65

The Five Year Old

I remember the day, years ago,
when my little brother refused to go to this stranger,
who came into town with his followers
like some ragged Roman legion.
Everyone spoke of him with such awe
that even though my brother didn't understand
what was said, he felt the import
and wanted nothing to do with a man with powers.
I did. When my father thrust me toward him,
I stared at his brown eyes as he held me up,
his men yelling at us to move away
and not to bother the master.
He quieted them, told them to let all the children come.
Then he breathed on my brow, kissed my cheeks,
blessed me with his hands that felt smooth with dust.
He then slipped a small pebble into my fist,
told me to keep it to remember him.
Years later, when I was old enough to go on my own,
I followed Peter to Rome, to a place where stones
formed temples and columns that put Jerusalem to shame.
I watched from a distance as Peter died,
crucified like the Christ, the Messiah,
the one who blessed me with his pebble
and set me on a journey over hard stones
with a rock for a companion.

The Rich Ruler

Some of what I own came from my father,
but most I bought through my shrewdness,
my knack for seeing a bargain and not hesitating.
I knew I found something precious in this man,
something I had not found before.
He knew what I needed to know
and told me what I must do to be justified
before the Lord. Sell everything,
give all to the poor and follow him.
I thought about my bed,
the mattress filled with feathers
from a thousand pigeons and chickens,
the pillow made from Egyptian cotton,
the blankets woven by Cappadocians.
Then I remembered my clothes from Rome,
the mosaics I brought back with me
from my time there,
the pewter plates on which my meals were served
by slaves from Libya who lived in my home,
the largest in my district,
with storehouses of grain and goat cheese,
olive oil and wine,
spices from each corner of the world.
I laughed at myself,
knowing that the tears I felt
flow to my chin would soon fall
on the dust of this place, my home,
which had a hold on me that was stronger
than any chain I could break, any weight I could lift.

The Blind Man

I almost wish he hadn't restored my sight.
Blind from birth, I never could imagine
what a face looked like looking at me,
the disgust in the grimace, the spit
shot from the side of the mouth to the hard ground.
Now I see the painted faces of the Pharisees
wondering how to kill the man who wished me well.
I see the lesions on the skin of my own arms
and on the once smooth necks and calves
of my own children, cursed with the devil's touch.
I see the mold in the squash, the curdle in the milk,
the sky turned gray scarred by lightning.
I see the stupid disbelief of these men
who follow the Nazarene to Jerusalem.
He speaks clearly; he tells his truth; he says he will die,
and their faces betray their slow minds and pride.
They refuse to be followers of a dead man
and tell him they don't understand.
I see. Now I see. The limp body hanging from a tree,
the blood flowing down his flayed back,
the soldiers laughing below his agony and shame,
and I wish my eyes could not see
the ordinary blight of this world,
the extraordinary grief of this day.

Zacchaeus

Racing with the boys through the street
with my small legs, I could never keep up.
They teased me, of course,
for being short and slow, so I took solace
in a different sort of stature,
aspiring to be feared. I saw how the tax collectors
walked the streets, immune from ridicule
by people afraid that they would be charged more
for their wagging tongues.
I befriended these men, learned their art,
the way of counting twice, of collecting
just enough for the temple and for myself.
I married, raised my sons to stand tall,
taught them to nurture fear in others.
But this never felt right.
As a boy, I would climb trees,
pretend to be tall, imagine flying
above the tiled roofs of Jericho homes.
When the master came to town,
I knew I had to see for myself
and raced ahead to the tree I often climbed,
I knew which branches made the best steps
to a place I could sit and rest
hidden by the wide leaves from those below.
But the Nazarene saw me through the blades of palm.
I avoided his gaze yet wanted to see his eyes.
He saw me, and I knew he tasted my shame.
When he called my name,
I heard the goodness in me I had almost drowned
in self-pity and rage.
Then I knew that I belonged here,
in this high place, at peace with myself,
my best self, recognized for what I could be
and what I still was, born of light and air,
ready to give away what dragged me down
and love myself,

even these stumps of legs that,
I now see, have carried me so well all these years.

V. The Arrival

The Caretaker of the Colt

Living so close to Jerusalem, just on the outskirts,
near Bethphage and Bethany,
close by the Mount of Olives,
my neighbors wondered over my extravagance,
buying a colt, one they assumed I would ride to town.
I had witnessed its birth.
It came into this world bathed in blood and water,
falling from its mother to the hay below.
I made an offer to the owner. I had fallen in love.
I knew nothing more beautiful than his white coat,
his black eyes and dancing legs.
I took it home and tethered it just outside my door,
Listening each night for thieves and boys eager to torture
anything that would sound its pain.
I knew, like all things I had ever loved, that it would not stay,
like my wife, who had died giving birth to my stillborn son.
I knew this colt was mine and not mine,
that a time would come when its purpose would reveal itself,
which is why I never rode it nor let my nephew,
eager to race through the streets, sit on its back.
When the two strangers came and untied it,
their answer to my question silenced me.
I knew the time had come both for it to leave
and for me to follow. After all, nothing held me here
other than habit. I joined with those
who lifted the master atop its back.
I even lent my cloak. I held the rope
on the long walk to Jerusalem, through the gate,
where so many waited with palm branches
hailing the hero they wanted, not the one who arrived
atop a white colt, speaking truth.

The Money Changer

I know my goodness, my worth, my place in this city.
I sacrifice in the temple and help others
spill the blood of pigeons, sheep,
even bulls for Rome, for Herod,
for the priests who invite me to dine at their homes,
as I host them at my table,
where we show all that we own
as a way of saying: This is who I am,
this is why we do business with each other,
the basis of the respect others owe us.
So when this upstart magic-maker
walked to me and saw my stall,
my guards and my posted rates of exchange,
I readied myself to make him a fair offer
so he could tell others of the advantages
of my business, my bargains, my prices.
The insult I felt when he kicked over the table,
my coins flying on the stones
to be clutched by beggars,
was nothing compared to the lashes
of his belt and tongue as he scolded me
for doing what the priests had commended me for:
scrupulousness to the law, cleanliness of hand,
prudential judgment in the furnishings of my home
and the conduct of my wife.
Calling the priests traitors to our people was bad enough,
but woe to those who are bad for business.
His tantrum in the marketplace would be the final act
of this dealer in pretense and hope.

The Tricksters

The day he arrived, we tried to trap him in the marketplace
just outside the temple where our questions
would lead to answers that would damn him
in our courts and in the hearts of the crowd.
Make no mistake. We played a game,
risking that blood would be spilled
by the swords of the Romans
who do not trust crowds
and who settle all conflict the same savage way.

First we asked about his sources:
In whose name did he come?
Who were his teachers?
What was his family beyond this Nazarene woman?
He played the game well and answered with a question,
as we all do, but one we could not answer:
"Who sent the Baptist?" We stayed silent,
knowing our words would damn us.
Then he told one of his stories,
the kind that crowds like.
They hung onto his words, waiting for the final line,
and laughed at us when it came,
comparing us to murderous tenant farmers.

So we made a new move, using deception,
hiring agents to pose as followers to ask a question
that he could not answer safely: Should we pay taxes?
The agents came back to us
impressed with his cleverness,
an answer that nearly turned them into followers.
He simply said: "Show me a coin.
Whose face does it wear?"
When they replied "Caesar's,"
he said to return to Caesar what belongs to him.

V. The Arrival

Once again, the crowd delighted in this back and forth,
this word-play that we knew he would soon lose
even if we had to buy someone
to put words in his mouth.
For us, the stakes are too high,
the matter not one of scripture but of practicality.
This man, simply, had to die.

The Spice Merchant

My shop is near the Temple,
so business has always been good,
people walking by my pyramids of cardamom,
nutmeg, cinnamon and turmeric,
the colors alone tempting buyers with taste
and scent of places they would never see.
So when this strange rabbi came down the street with his hosannas
and ragged band of Galileans listening to his dangerous words,
his talk of end-times, enslavement,
exile and betrayal, I knew this would be bad for business.
Who wants to spend money on spice
if they believe their world is ending?
The more I listened, though, the less I worried;
a strange peace descended as I imagined my death,
my bones and flesh wrapped in linens
scented by my own spices
and placed in some cave where I would wait
for roots of trees to descend and enter my world,
my corpse, drawing something from me
to help them live as my flesh melted, leaving only
dry bones and dust that nothing could harm:
I imagined this as he spoke, and when he left,
my spices began to bore me with scents
all too familiar, colors I had seen too often,
and I almost hoped for a time when the walls would shake,
upsetting all I knew and giving me a chance
to start over, afresh, weighed down by nothing,
as the wind blew me away, like a fine spray of salt.

VI. The Passion

The Host

I chose to live here, near Gethsemane
because of the olive trees,
their trunks as twisted and wayward
as a prayer's circuitous route skyward;
their fruit as bitter and satisfying
as God's reply to our inarticulate cry for comfort.
I furnished the upstairs room with couches
to make this a place of prayer
for Passover visitors traveling from places
beyond the walls of this holy city.
I wanted it far from the bloodbath of the temple
but close enough to the market to purchase
the lamb, the herbs, the bread
to mark the time when God gave us little warning
that our freedom was to come
with a midnight run across a dry seabed.

I was pleased when my servant returned
from the well with his full pitcher
trailing behind him these strangers,
disciples of the master. They rented my room
for their celebration. I crouched near the door
to listen to something new—a Passover
like none I had ever witnessed.
He blessed everything with the music of his words
as he broke the bread and passed the wine,
each crumb and drop a part of himself.
He singled out one impurity:
a man who would betray him.
He chastised all for arguing over their place,
telling them something I knew in my heart:
stay low to the ground, like the olive tree:
take time to grow and bear fruit, and do so
quietly, subtly, covered in the gray dust
of the morning road.

VI. The Passion

When he went to the garden to pray,
the dust of the night mingled with his tears and prayers.
I kept watch while the others slept
Fatigued by confusion and fear.
When the temple guards came,
led by the betrayer, I whispered a prayer
for this man who had blessed my house forever
with his meal, with his words, with his sorrow.

The Temple Servant

I wash the blood from the stones
after the sacrifices and bring the meat
to the priests for their dinner and for sale
in the markets, which is forbidden,
but I do so anyway, as the temple
is the law and above the law.
When I was told to fetch the silver
to pay the betrayer, I did so.
I know my place: to obey,
to diminish myself in the commands handed to me.
I walked at night with the guards and priests
to the Mount of Olives
and saw the surprise of the men we waylaid
in the shadows of the trees,
in the shelter of the garden walls.
We knew they might be armed,
but when the moonlight flashed on the blade,
I was stunned and frozen like a statue,
barely moving as the sword took off my ear
in one stroke. I held my hand to the
tangle of blood and hair
and fought to stifle my scream,
when this man they call the master pulled my hand away
and cupped my ear as if to tell me
I was a beloved son.
I felt no more warmth of blood,
only the flesh returned
and a sense that I should listen
only to myself, to the steady beat
of my own heart and, from this point on,
what it commands me to do.

The Woman in the Shadows

Even the faint light of the oil lamp
worries me at night around the temple.
I prefer being in the dark places
behind the columns and in the alleys
watching others, waiting to see signs
of weakness and worry so I can point my finger
and name the demons that others hide.
I've done this since I was a girl,
fearing the words of others judging me,
seeing my weakness and failure.
When the guards brought this zealot
to judge him, I breathed easy for a bit,
even easier when his follower came,
reeking of Galilee, his tongue betraying his tribe.
The trick is not to accuse at first,
but to question: Aren't you his friend,
even the leader of his men?
His words meant nothing. Only the panic
flashing in his eyes as he denied and denied
over and over, until a rooster warned us
that light would come and reveal us to ourselves.
That's when this man's face became a mirror,
and I saw a glimpse of my own panic,
the betrayal I had made
back when I was a girl
giving into fear, denying who I was.
I wept then and still feel heartsick,
refusing to believe either the world or I
can ever change.

The Torturer

When I was a child, I learned quickly
when to set my face to stone and when to cringe
from the fists of my father and the leather belt
he would use to whip me. Sometimes he wanted to see the fear
flashing across my eyes. Then he would stop.
At other times, that fear only excited him more
as he broke my bones and bled my flesh
of fear. I learned from him and tried to teach my own son
that fear breeds respect. But he ran off,
unwilling to endure further lessons.
The scribes saw my skill, my disdain for weakness,
my ability to read the horror in others.
So when they told me and my men
that this man was a prophet,
we knew what to do. After we applied the blindfold
and bound his hands, we spun him round
and cracked his ribs and head with our clubs
shouting at him to tell us our names
and who laid the blow. He stayed silent.
And when I took off his blindfold,
I looked to see what kind of man he was:
one who blinked or one who stared back.
He did neither. I don't know what he did.
Was it a smile? A prayer?
A sigh for someone else?
When I struck him full on his cheek
with my fist, cracking a bone,
he fell and then stood and continued his trance,
not willing to play our game.
He took all the fun away,
and when the guards took him to his cell,
I laughed with my men at the joke we played
on this prophet, this teacher, this half a man,
whose face stays with me to this day
and the feel of his flesh on my fist,
stinging me still.

Joseph of Arimathea

I knew some of the priests since we were boys
studying the Torah, following the laws
that governed our lives; laws that told us
what kind of men we were.
But I could see in their faces more
than the Torah could ever tell
of these former friends who now cared more about
standing in the light of Pilate and Herod,
dancing between their shadows,
while seeing what they could gain along the way.
I knew the lies they told, the fear that kept them
from reading the Torah the way I read the words
of prophets who once walked among my ancestors.
That's what I saw in the Nazarene.
Something that reminded me of Elijah, but new,
nothing like those false prophets in the marketplace.
I argued against his arrest. At the trial,
I knew I held no sway; no words
would turn the twisted heads of
the men whose title I shared,
to whose tribe I no longer felt I belonged.

I followed the Nazarene to Herod's palace.
The fool that I am, I thought I might tell Herod the truth.
He only wanted magic tricks,
something to break his boredom before he broke this Jesus in two.
When the prophet would not perform,
Herod sent him back; I watched Herod
sink into himself, his corpulence, his disdain
for anything that did not shine with power or newness,
that failed to delight a mind past any light or love.

I followed the Nazarene to Pilate.
I have heard the stories of this Roman's reluctance,
of his offering up of Barabbas,
of his pleading with the people

and his discernment that Jesus was an innocent.
I saw what transpired. Pilate was ready
to crucify us all. He saw in us only rebels
and, in Jesus, a man who might be king.
He signed the order in between
bites of skewered lamb, laughing
about something inconsequential to a young girl.

I followed the Nazarene to the whipping post
where guards tied his hands and lashed his back
flaying his skin into wet shreds of flesh,
more blood than meat or bone,
the thorns formed into a crown,
pounded into his head so it would stick
no matter how many times he fell
as he carried the two timbers to the place
they call the skull.

They drafted a foreigner, chosen for his dark skin,
to speed along this parade. The Romans wanted to return
to their drinking and gambling and eyeing
our girls with loneliness and lust.
They dispatched their duties with speed:
nails through the wrists and feet for Jesus
and two rebels: men who deserved to die.
Within three hours, it was over.
The guards wanted Jesus dead,
so the guards thrust a spear into his ribs
to let the air out of his lungs,
keep him from breathing more
of the fetid air of this high place.

Knowing his death was foregone
made me impatient, I confess, for the end.
I wanted it over, for my sake. For his.
For his mother's, who wept like no one
I have ever heard weep before.
A sound I shall never surrender.

VI. THE PASSION

A shattering of her soul like a seashell
on the rocks near Jaffa.
I wept for her, for me, for the place we were,
a world where we tore love from our hearts
and nailed it to dead wood to watch it bleed out.

I wanted to die. I wanted to lay beside him
in my own tomb. I paid the guards to move him.
They demanded more and then pried out the nails.
But they had mothers, too, and seeing his mother bent in pain,
they did not let him fall.
They carried him down,
though they were drained of energy,
as if they had died too.
One guard hoisted him below his arms;
another held his waist. A third gripped
his bloody legs and bleeding feet.
They set him down to push the stone away
and then left the hard part to the women—
to make him clean enough to give back to God:
to wash his body, perfume it with spices,
wrap him in new linen so tight he looked
like a swaddled infant, ready for a new birth
to someplace I both long for and fear,
a place where death lives.

VII. The Return

Mary, Mother of James

The two who have become my sisters
and I spent the night grieving with Mary,
who slept as if she were as dead as her son.
We could not sleep, but spent the last hours
gathering the spices and singing softly to ourselves
the psalms that Jesus had us sing at night
in the inns and when we camped below the night sky.
The dark was just turning blue when we left,
the stars still hovering, as we gathered our strength
to walk the way once again,
not far from the hill of his torment and passing.
We debated ways to roll back the stone.
Joanna began looking for a thick branch.
Mary Magdala kept watching for a farmer
on his way to market, one generous enough
to delay his sales for a few minutes.
We saw nothing, except, as we approached,
a glow that could not have been the dawn,
coming from the cave's open mouth,
the stone already pushed aside.
Joanna was the first to look inside,
and when she gasped, we both bent our heads
and then shaded our eyes from two men
who shone like lightning that had flashed and stayed,
dancing in place. They asked us what we were doing
as we stared at the folded linens and little else.
They laughed at us, not with contempt,
but the way a father does when he holds a child
and answers a simple question: Don't you know?
they asked us. Don't you remember what he said?
And they repeated Jesus's own words. Then we knew.
He was not here. He had risen
beyond our doubts, though we still dared to doubt
before risking belief. We left the spices,
their scent still sweet in our heads,
and walked and then ran as if we were girls

hurrying to men waiting for us.
I longed to tell my son the news I did not understand—
my son whom I warned at first
not to follow anyone, let alone a worker of miracles.

We arrived out of breath, the men just waking,
and we spoke all at once, struggling
to make ourselves understood
between gulps of air.
When we finally made our story plain,
we heard laughter again, but this time,
it stung. My own son called me hysterical.
The others wondered at our sanity,
blaming our visions on lack of sleep.
Some dared to call us gossips—
all but Peter, who said nothing.
He looked into each of our eyes,
searching for something he hoped was true.
When he found it, he raced outside,
ran with his bare and hairy legs,
retracing our path and returning
to tell our story back to us.
Only then did the others stop laughing
and begin starting on their own road
to the mouth of the cave
and the bright truth of a story
we still barely knew.

Cleopas

We had to leave, even after hearing the stories
the women had told and Peter had confirmed.
The city disgusted us with hypocrisy
that tasted like bile, priests who cared more
about keeping the Romans happy
and staying in power than feeling the freedom
that came from listening to the words
and seeing what the man from Nazareth did each day.
Always something new, like rising from the dead.
But the stink of the city stung our nostrils,
the noise of the streets made us long for the road.
We walked to Emmaus, a small town
with a good inn, just to clear our heads.
My companion spoke of cause and effect
as we debated who to blame:
the fickle citizens, the Romans or the priests.
We passed dozens of travelers on the road,
and we nodded to them; they did the same:
the sign that none of us were robbers.
So when this man came to us from behind,
we invited him to walk with us, knowing
three were stronger than two.
When he asked us what we had been saying,
we wondered where he had been hiding
these past days and nights. Everyone in Jerusalem
had been consumed by the news of his death
and the rumors of his appearance.
When we wondered aloud at the stories,
he laughed, and explained them
using the stories the master had told these past three years:
of Moses, Elijah, Isaiah, Ezekiel and the words
they used to point to this moment and that hill.
When the inn appeared before us, he made to move on.
We begged him to stay. He agreed,
and we sat to eat a simple meal.
Before the fish came, he took the bread,

held it high, said the blessing, and tore it in three pieces.
The light bathed him now anew, and we knew it was him.
We saw and understood, and as we did,
we looked at each other to seek confirmation
that what we saw was real and true.
When we looked again, he was gone
like a vision glimpsed sideways by a glancing eye.
We paid for our uneaten meal and made for Jerusalem,
running the whole way, even at night,
with no concern for thieves,
carrying news that could not wait
and that we had to share with the men and women
who already knew and wanted to know more
in the morning light of a new Jerusalem.

VII. The Return

Untitled

It wasn't death I feared so much as life,
the face of the traitor at the moment of betrayal;
the dull sword thrust below my ribs,
the cast nails hammered into my wrist,
the hollow taste of hunger in my gut and throat.

When I walked in, I smelled the sweetness of the coals
and the rosemary on the singed meat below the scales
and felt hungry for the moment the fish slid down the river
the first time, breathing in water and sunlight.

I knew he was not a ghost when he sat to eat.
I had no need to see the wounds
or trace the edges of his scars.

I felt more than alive, more in love
than any one person could make me feel,
loving them all more than I could ever love a brother or betrothed.
I felt as if I could wed the world, embracing it as my own.

He made us feel at peace, seeing him whole and holy,
his skin glowing with a shine full of morning and candlelight.
We knew death could only sting for a flash of a moment.
Later, we would look like him, smiling and alive.

When I walked to Bethany, they all followed
singing hymns that named the plants and animals of the first garden
as if to unnerve the universe and create it anew.

I still doubt, though I knew at the time what I saw
and what it meant. I suspect my doubts
will make me question what my eyes saw and heart felt
that evening in Jerusalem when he stayed for a moment
before going somewhere else, leaving me with the beautiful burden
of his call to be still, to watch for the flame of grace
to dance over my head and whisper
to me—to us: *You are loved.*

Afterword

With this poetic retelling of The Gospel of Luke, I hope I have provided a new lens with which to view familiar stories and have breathed some new meaning into the story of Jesus. The poems, ones that re-envision gospel stories as intimate news relayed by close friends, bring both humanity and immediacy to the gospels to help readers approach them as if for the first time. Ultimately, this work seeks to give a human face to Jesus along the lines of other artists and writers over the centuries who have worked to lift Christ out of iconic mythology and bring him back to his human origins and restore the power of his stories and journeys.

This work was informed by my many years of reading and writing poems about a man whose stories have become easy tropes. I hope those who read it will approach religion and spirituality in a new way, one not rooted in dogma or tradition, but in the spirit of relationship that the common people had with Jesus. As the world divides itself along dangerous lines, pitting belief systems against each other, I hope my work reminds us of all—Moslems from Ramallah, Baptists from Indianapolis, Buddhists from Singapore or Hindus from New Delhi—of our shared humanity. We are all rooted in similar stories and in the same spirit, regardless of the nuances of time, place and tradition.

My work, I also hope, extends the new wave of literature about Christ. I am especially indebted to Reza Azlan's *Zealot: The Life and Times of Jesus of Nazareth* and to Ron Hansen's *Atticus,* which is modern retelling of the Prodigal Son parable. This book is also part of an older tradition of gospel translations, including Nikos Kazantzakis's *The Last Temptation of Christ* (which Martin Scorsese turned into a film), T.S. Eliot's "Journey of the Magi" and Khalil Gibran's *The Prophet.*

I hope that as you read this work, something stirred in you. Perhaps you sensed a spirit at once your own and part of something larger. Perhaps you sensed a person and personality beyond the art of Byzantium or Florence. If so, then I have succeeded in what I set out to do: to add color and definition and depth to a remarkable person we barely know and whose lessons we still struggle to understand.

Acknowledgements

I am indebted first and foremost to my friend and brother-in-Christ Brian McCaffery for his careful editing of these poems. Both a gifted ornithologist and a deacon, he brought both a religious and scientific sensibility to his edits that made this work far stronger.

Years ago, I studied Dante's *Divine Comedy* in Italy with Ron Herzman of SUNY Geneseo through a grant from the National Endowment for the Humanities. He, along with the other teachers in our seminar, taught me to read Dante in a way that forever shaped my own writing.

Thanks also go to the late Stan Rice, my first poetry instructor at San Francisco State University, where I pursued my master's degree in fine arts. His first assignment was to have us write a series of poems that made up one long work. That 27-page work gave me the confidence that I could embark on a longer poetic journey.

As this work was shaped by my experience of the Spiritual Exercises of St. Ignatius of Loyola, I also have him to thank, as well as Fr. Anthony P. Sauer, S.J., my former boss and my spiritual director when I undertook the exercises back in 2003. He is the best boss I've ever had and most likely ever will have.

Thanks also go to Fr. John Mossi, S.J., who first introduced me to Ignatian prayer and to the remarkable poetry of Gerard Manley Hopkins, S.J., a priest and poet who has been my poetic muse since I first picked up his slim collection of poetry.

I am also grateful to the good folks at Wipf and Stock who chose this book for publication. I hope they continue publishing books in a time when print publishing is suffering from the desire by so many for free online content.

Finally, I thank my family, especially my wife, Kathryn, for her love and companionship. She has taught me to be a kinder, more loving person than the young man she married, and I am grateful to her for her patience and trust in me.